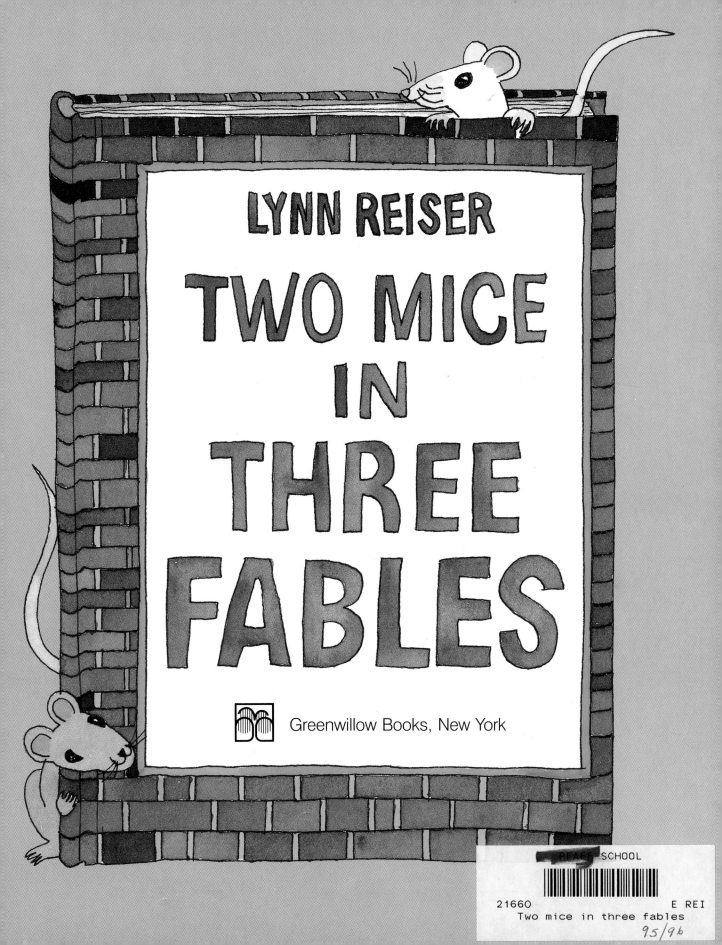

LYNN REISER

TWO MICE
IN
THREE
FABLES

Greenwillow Books, New York

For
one Susan
who found
two mice
and
two Susans
who found
one snake

Watercolor paints and a black pen
were used for the full-color art.
The text type is Helvetica Light.

Greenwillow Books, a division of William Morrow &
Company, Inc., 1350 Avenue of the Americas,
New York, NY 10019.

Printed in Hong Kong by South China Printing
Company (1988) Ltd.
First Edition   10 9 8 7 6 5 4 3 2 1

Library of Congress Cataloging-in-Publication Data
Two mice in three fables / by Lynn Reiser.
    p.   cm.
Summary: Three stories featuring various animal characters,
including two mice, present simple lessons for life.
ISBN 0-688-13389-4 (trade).   ISBN 0-688-13390-8 (lib. bdg.)
1. Fables.   2. Children's stories, American. [1. Fables.
2. Animals—Fiction.] I. Title.   II. Title: 2 mice in 3 fables.
PZ8.2.R3535Tw   1995   [E]—dc20
93-35935   CIP   AC

CONTENTS

 TWO MICE

page 4

 THE OWL AND THE RACCOON

page 12

 THE QUICK SLICK SNAKE

page 22

1
TWO MICE

Once there were two mice
who lived beside a window.

One lived

inside the window,

in a cage

on top of a bookshelf.

One lived

outside the window,

in a mouse hole

under a rosebush.

The inside mouse

ate mouse food from a bowl,

drank water from a bottle,

and ran around a wheel.

  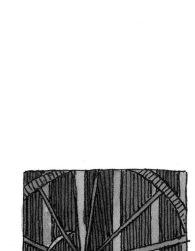

The outside mouse
ate strawberries
and acorns,
drank raindrops
from rose leaves,
and ran
in and out
the mouse hole
and up and down
and around
the rosebush.

One night
the window was open.
The outside mouse ran in.

The two mice

ate mouse food from the bowl,

drank water from the bottle,

and ran around the wheel.

One mouse

was

content.

One mouse

was

ready for more.

The outside mouse ran out.

The inside mouse followed.

The two mice

ate a strawberry—

and a snake almost ate them.

They nibbled

an acorn—

and a raccoon

almost nibbled them.

They drank raindrops

from a rose leaf—

and an owl

almost carried them

off to her nest.

 One mouse

was ready for more.

One mouse

was ready for a nap.

The window was open.
The inside mouse ran in.

The outside mouse
did not follow.
The outside mouse ran
in and out
and up and down
and around,
playing
"catch me if you can"
with the snake
and the raccoon
and the owl.

The inside mouse
took a nap.

2

THE OWL AND THE RACCOON

Once there were an owl and a raccoon
who always wanted to be in the same place.

When it was nesting time,

the owl picked
a deep hole high in a tree
to build a nest
for her owlets.

The raccoon picked
a deep hole high in a tree
to build a nest
for her cubs.

It was the same hole.

The raccoon got there first.

The owl had to nest in a hole

on the other side of the tree.

When the owl's owlets were too big

for the hole in the tree,

the owl wanted to teach them to fly.

The owl picked a wide limb

for her owlets to perch on.

When the raccoon's cubs were too big

for the hole in the tree,

the raccoon wanted to move them

to a den under a stone wall.

The raccoon picked a wide limb

for her cubs to walk down.

It was the same limb.

The owl got there first.
The raccoon
and her cubs
had to slide down
a limb
on the other side
of the tree.

One night
the owl
and the raccoon
and the owl's owlets
and the raccoon's cubs
were hungry.

The owl flew around,
looking around.

The owl saw two mice walking.

The owl watched the mice.

She perched

in the top of the tree,

waiting.

Then she balanced

at the edge of the roof,

watching and waiting.

The raccoon prowled around,

looking around.

The raccoon saw two mice walking.

The raccoon watched the mice.

She crouched behind the stone wall,

waiting.

She crawled under the rosebush,

watching and waiting.

When the mice
walked by,
the owl swooped,
the raccoon
pounced.

It was the same two mice.

The owl _and_ the raccoon

got there first.

The owl caught the raccoon.

The raccoon caught the owl.

The mice
walked on.

The owl's owlets ate bugs.

The raccoon's cubs ate acorns.

The owl and the raccoon
ate fur and feathers.

MORAL
Take turns or
tempt trouble.

3
THE QUICK SLICK SNAKE

Once there was a quick slick snake

who lived in a stone wall.

The snake liked to lick spiders off windowsills,

steal eggs out of birds' nests,

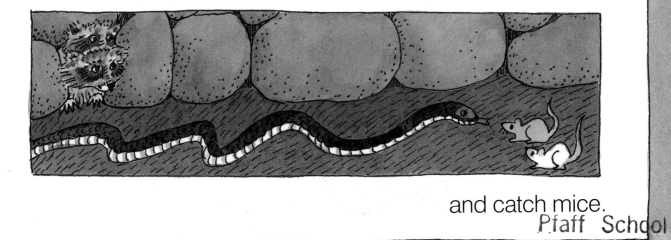

and catch mice.

One night

the snake was lying in the grass,

pretending to be a stick.

Two mice walked by.

The snake shot

straight at the mice.

But

one mouse hopped up,

one mouse dropped down.

The snake slid straight—

and the mice walked on.

One night
the snake was draped
over a branch,
studying a bird's nest.
Two mice walked by.
It was the same two mice.

The quick snake
hopped up
and
dropped down.
But
one mouse bounced backward,
one mouse flipped forward.

The snake sprawled—

and the mice walked on.

One night

the snake was shedding its skin

in the rosebush.

Two mice walked by.

The slick snake

bounced backward,

then

flipped forward

at the mice.

But

one mouse rolled right,

one mouse lunged left.

The snake somersaulted—

and the mice walked on.

The next night

the snake

watched and waited

until the two mice walked by.

The snake
wound itself
higher and higher,
tighter and tighter,
and—

bounced
backward
and
flipped
forward,
lunged
left
and
rolled
right,
hopped
up
and
dropped
down,

and—

The mice stood still.

The snake

twisted

and tangled

and tied.

The mice

watched

and waited.

HISS

The snake

untied

and untangled

and untwisted.

The snake slouched away

to lick spiders.

And the mice walked on.

MORAL

Today's trick is
tomorrow's tangle.